A Splinter

Ben Brown lives in London. His plays include *Four Letter Word* (Edinburgh Fringe; Cameron Mackintosh New Writing Award); *All Things Considered* (Stephen Joseph Theatre, Hampstead Theatre, Petit Théâtre de Paris, Marian Street Theatre, Sydney, Zimmertheater, Heidelberg); *Larkin With Women* (Stephen Joseph Theatre, West Yorkshire Playhouse, Coventry Belgrade, Manchester Library Theatre, Orange Tree Theatre; Express Play of the Year, TMA Best New Play); *The Promise* (Orange Tree Theatre); and *Three Days in May* (national tour and West End; Whatsonstage Best New Play).

BEN BROWN

A Splinter of Ice

faber

First published in 2021
by Faber and Faber Limited
74–77 Great Russell Street
London WC1B 3DA

Typeset by Brighton Gray
Printed and bound in the UK by CPI Group (Ltd), Croydon CR0 4YY

A CIP record for this book
is available from the British Library

978-0-571-37138-9

2 4 6 8 10 9 7 5 3 1

Introduction

Some time in 2014 I was reading Yvonne Cloetta's memoir of her life with Graham Greene when I came across a chapter dealing with his relationship with the notorious Soviet spy Kim Philby, who she described as the 'one man for whom Graham committed himself totally'.

This sparked my interest as I knew about Greene and I knew about Philby but I didn't know that they'd been friends (ever since Greene had worked under Philby at MI6 during the war). Or that Greene had been the only person to defend Philby after he defected to Russia in 1963. Or that Greene had been to see him in Moscow in the late 1980s, thus satisfying Philby's long-standing, publicly stated desire 'to sit across a table from Graham Greene with a bottle of wine between us'.

Of that meeting in February 1987, all Greene was prepared to say to his biographer was that 'we had a private dinner. I went by myself to his flat but I won't say anything about that.' Which felt like an invitation to imagine.

I finished the play the following year but for various reasons (not least, of course, the global pandemic) it was programmed and postponed several times before reaching this point, for which I'm indebted to the determination and ingenuity of the indefatigable Alastair Whatley.

No play I've written has had such a tortuous journey to the stage and I consider myself very lucky in these dark days of Covid-19 to be finally seeing it produced.

Ben Brown

To my parents

With thanks to Alan and Oliver

A Splinter of Ice was filmed at Everyman Theatre, Cheltenham, and had its online premiere on 15 April 2021, with the following cast:

Graham Greene Oliver Ford Davies
Kim Philby Stephen Boxer
Rufa Philby Sara Crowe

Director Alan Strachan
Co-Director Alastair Whatley
Designer Michael Pavelka
Lighting Designer Jason Taylor
Sound Designer and Composer Max Pappenheim
Casting Director Ellie Collyer-Bristow CDG
Costume Supervisor Siobhan Boyd
Props Supervisor Robyn Hardy
Production Manager Tammy Rose
Company Stage Manager Paul Ferris
Deputy Stage Manager Felix Dunning

For Original Theatre:
Artistic Director Alastair Whatley
Creative Producer Tom Hackney
Head of Marketing Emma Martin
Marketing Co-ordinator Rachel McCall
Assistant Producer Sam Harding

Characters

Graham Greene
Kim Philby
Rufa Philby

Setting

Kim Philby's flat in Moscow
on the evening of 15th February 1987

A SPLINTER OF ICE

'Our interest's on the dangerous edge of things.
The honest thief, the tender murderer . . .'

Robert Browning

Act One

'The Harry Lime Theme' from The Third Man *as the house lights go down and the audience settles.*

Then a spot catches the face of a man standing in the shadows wearing a black trilby hat and a thick black winter coat with the collar turned up, just like the famous image in the film.

But on closer inspection this man is older, much older, and is in fact the film's author, Graham Greene.

He smiles enigmatically, Harry Lime-style.

The music fades.

Pause.

Graham Just don't ask me any questions.

He takes his hat off.

That was almost the first thing he said to me . . . which wasn't the best start to the evening . . . especially if, like me, you were looking for answers.

He reflects.

And he must have known how much I'd been looking forward to the full, uncensored story at last, told in person by the greatest spy of the twentieth century.

Beat.

So perhaps he was simply playing with me . . . as he had played with so many others . . .

He thinks.

One never really knew with Kim.

Pause.
Then the lights come up to reveal Kim Philby
(seventies but still handsome) wearing a jacket and tie.
They look at each other for a moment.

Kim Well, I can see a lot of water has passed by. You're looking a good deal older.

He waits for a reaction.

Graham No more than you.

They smile and embrace, a little awkwardly.
Then separate.

Kim How long has it been?

Graham Thirty-five years, I reckon.

Kim Probably . . .

Beat.

Please though . . . just don't ask me any questions.

Graham takes this in.

Graham I will ask you just one . . .

Beat.

How is your Russian?

Kim smiles.

Kim Not bad.

An attractive woman in her mid-fifties steps forward. She speaks with a Russian accent.

Rufa Terrible.

They laugh.
An ice-breaker.

Kim Graham, this is Rufa. Rufa, Graham.

Graham How do you do.

They shake hands.

Rufa I am very happy to meet you. I have never met any of Kim's English friends before.

Beat.

Kim Here, come in from the cold.

They go inside and the lights cross-fade to reveal the hall and living room of the flat. There is an upright chair, some coat hooks and a radiator.
Rufa takes Graham's hat and coat and hangs them up.

Rufa Please, take your shoes off and I will dry them for you.

Graham Thank you. Yes, I forgot to bring any boots.

Rufa That is very bad. In Moscow in February you must have boots.

Graham Yes.

He sits down and bends down slowly to take off his shoes.

Rufa Here, let me help you.

Graham Well, you needn't.

Rufa It's no problem. I do yours, don't I, Kim?

Kim (*a little embarrassed*) Well . . . sometimes.

She helps him with his shoes.

Graham You speak very good English.

Rufa Yes. I learnt it from reading your books.

She smiles.

And from Kim, of course, whose Russian is –

Kim You said.

She takes Graham's shoes to the radiator.

Rufa Now, how about your socks?

Graham (*quickly*) They're fine. Really.

Rufa Very well.

She picks up some slippers.

Here, put Kim's slippers on.

She gives them to him.

Graham Thank you.

He puts them on.

Rufa Good. Now you boys go and have a nice chat while I get dinner ready.

She goes off into the kitchen.

Kim When she moved in, I told her the kitchen was my patch, but today she insisted . . . Anyway, do come through.

Kim leads the way into the living room.
There is a green wingback chair, right, another armchair, left, and a sofa facing us, all arranged around a low table. On the back wall above the sofa is a print of a Roman emperor (sent by Anthony Blunt), a pair of duelling pistols and a pair of bear skins. There is also a Festival radio with a small wooden chair next to it and a record player next to the green wingback chair.
Graham looks at a photograph in a frame on the wall.

Graham What's this?

Kim turns.

Oh, sorry. I wasn't meant to ask you any questions, was I?

Kim smiles.

Kim You can ask me that.

He looks at the photograph.

That's me with the Dynamo Moscow Ice Hockey Team.
I was asked to be their 'motivational manager' before the
European Championships.

Graham How did they get on?

Kim They lost their next four games . . . Vodka?

Graham Please.

Kim fixes the drinks as Graham takes in the room.

So, tell me about Rufa. If you don't mind my asking.

Kim What do you want to know?

Graham Well, how did you meet her?

Kim At an ice show, actually. She was a friend of a friend.

Graham Ah . . .

Kim seems reluctant to say more.

Kim And how's . . . (*He searches for her name.*) Yvonne,
isn't it?

Graham Yes. Well, thank you.

Kim Good.

Graham She sends her regards.

Kim Thank you. Send mine back.

Graham I will.

*Kim gives Graham his drink.
Then raises his glass.*

Kim Anyway, to your health.

Graham Yes. And yours.

Graham raises his.

Kim And friendship.

Graham Yes.

They drink.

Kim Do sit down.

Graham Thank you.

Graham sits on the sofa, Kim on the green wingback chair.

Kim So you're here for the Peace Conference?

Graham Yes. Or to be precise, 'for a nuclear-free world and the survival of humanity' . . . I felt I couldn't really say no to that.

Kim No . . . And how is the Hotel Cosmos? As good as they say?

Graham I don't know what they say, but it's full of cockroaches. And other dodgy characters.

Kim smiles.

Kim They built it to impress the Americans, you know. At the 1980 Olympics. But then they never turned up.

Graham Yes . . . because of Afghanistan, wasn't it?

Kim I believe so. Rather the pot calling the kettle, don't you think?

Graham You could say that . . . Anyway, there are a lot of Americans there now.

Kim Oh yes, who?

Graham Well, I've seen Gregory Peck, wearing a name card . . . Shirley Maclaine . . . and Norman Mailer, who cemented a peace pact with Gore Vidal over dinner.

Kim Well, I guess that's a start.

Graham Yes . . . There's also a singer called Kris Kristofferson, Claudia Cardinale, still looking stunning, and

amongst the English contingent, Fay Weldon, in place of an
absent Iris Murdoch, and Peter Ustinov.

Kim Oh yes? His father was one of my agents as it happens.

Graham (*surprised*) Really?

Kim During the war I mean.

Graham Ah . . .

　Beat.

Oh, and I saw Yoko Ono kiss Gorbachev.

Kim Ah yes, Gorbachev . . . He's the man we've been
waiting for.

Graham You've met him, have you?

Kim . . . Sadly not.

Graham Oh. Well, I met him today, actually.

　Kim is impressed.

Only briefly though. Before the main meeting.

Kim And what did he say?

Graham He said he had known me for some time . . .

Kim Through your books?

Graham Yes . . . (*Suddenly doubtful.*) At least, I assume
that's what he meant . . .

Kim Yes, I'm sure he did. Anyway, that's nice, isn't it?

Graham I thought so. After all, that's how I want people to
know me, for the most part. Present company excepted.

　Kim smiles.

And there were lots of journalists, of course. So I know what
you mean about not wanting to answer any questions. They
kept shoving tape-recorders in my face and bombarding me

with questions like 'How do you like our Glasnost and Perestroika?' 'What do you think of Gorbachev?' 'What is your attitude to the Pope?' 'What are your views on religion?'

Kim And what did you say?

Graham I want to pee.

Kim Oh, of course. It's through there on the left.

Graham No, I said that to them.

Kim Oh.

Pause.

Anyway, I'm very touched you found time to come and see me.

Graham Well, of course I did. I've been wanting to for years.

Kim So have I. But I'd pretty much lost hope you ever would. And obviously I couldn't come to you.

Graham No . . .

Beat.

Kim Good old Gorby then, for getting us together.

Graham Yes . . .

He hesitates.

But the truth is, I very nearly didn't see you.

Kim Why?

Graham Because I wasn't sure you would want to see me.

Kim But I told everyone I wanted to share a bottle of wine with you.

Graham Yes, but that was before that journalist spilt the beans about me showing your letters to MI6.

Kim Oh . . . yes.

Graham And you haven't written since. So, I suppose I'm trying to say, sorry about that . . . But you know what it's like. One never really leaves the firm . . .

Kim I did.

Graham Yes, well, unless you join another one I mean.

Kim . . . It's quite all right. There's no need to apologise.

Graham I didn't get you into hot water here, did I?

Kim No. More warm, I'd call it. And, of course, you don't for a moment think I didn't show your letters to my people?

Graham No. But you didn't make it public.

Kim Yes, well, not a lot is made public in the USSR.

He smiles.

Have another vodka.

Graham Thank you.

Kim refills their glasses.
    A thought strikes Graham.

This place isn't bugged, is it?

Kim smiles.

Kim Good Lord, no . . . You don't think they'd bother with a couple of old fogies like us, do you?

Graham No, I suppose not. But it just occurred to me it might be.

Kim No . . .

Beat.

It used to be, I think, but that was before the new regime.

Graham Perestroika and Glasnost you mean?

Kim No, I meant the cuts. But I suppose it's the other side of the same coin really. They can't afford to do much spying any more. All that listening takes up an enormous amount of manpower you know. Even if the bugs were still in place.

Graham And are they?

He looks around the room.

Kim Who knows? But I shouldn't worry about it. I never do . . . It's pure vanity to think anyone still cares about me.

He drinks.

But I must admit, Rufa was a bit fazed when she first realised we were being watched. In the early days, I'm talking about.

Graham What happened?

Kim Well, it was all because of the loo paper.

Graham Loo paper?

Kim Yes. We were in a restaurant once when my daughter was visiting from England. And Rufa went to the Ladies and found there was a roll of paper in it.

Graham What's so strange about that?

Kim They don't have loo paper in restaurants here, except those reserved for tourists and the KGB. Everyone else brings their own. So it was then she finally realised we were being followed and the shady character in the corner was actually our benefactor, as it were. And it was all done so that my daughter wouldn't take the story of Russian deprivation back to England.

Graham takes this in.

Graham Yes, well, come to think of it, I don't think I've ever been caught short here either.

Kim Of course not. A world famous author like yourself. It wouldn't do. And I'm sure they stretch to loo paper at the Cosmos in any case. Full of tourists, you see.

Graham And the KGB.

Kim Very probably.

They drink.

Graham Tell me more about your life here . . .

Kim hesitates.

You notice that wasn't a question.

Kim Yes. But I rather think it was.

Graham smiles.

Graham Describe an average day for me, that's all I want
to know.

Kim thinks.

Kim Very well.

Beat.

I get up and make myself a cup of tea, and then sit in that
chair – (*He points to the small wooden chair.*) listening to
the BBC World Service news . . . Then I have breakfast and
read *Izvestia*, before taking the short walk to the post office
to get my post, including my next several-days-out-of-date
copy of *The Times*, which I'm mainly interested in for the
football and cricket scores and the crossword. The rest
strikes me as pure propaganda.

Graham And the Russian papers aren't?

Kim I didn't say that.

Beat.

Graham What about the afternoon?

Kim Well, I now take very seriously my doctor's advice to
take it easy. So after lunch I usually take a nap, and then a
gentle stroll to wake me up, before coming back here to
read for a while.

Graham In English or Russian?

Kim English.

Graham Where do you get the books?

Kim Where I've got them since I was an undergraduate. Bowes and Bowes in Cambridge. Though they've recently changed their name to Sherratt and Hughes, which I wrote and told them was rather a shock to a conservative like me . . .

   Beat.

Of course, there's a large English language library at the British Council but they've closed their doors to me alas. As have the Americans. Understandable, I suppose . . .

Graham And do you go out to the theatre? Or the cinema?

Kim Not much. My Russian isn't really good enough, so Rufa tends to go with a friend. But I like going to the Bolshoi, or to concerts sometimes. Though I don't like it when Western journalists try to talk to me . . .

Graham What about work?

Kim Ah . . . now you're straying into forbidden territory. But I don't think it's any great secret to say I'm mostly retired now. Though I still give the odd lecture.

Graham Lecture?

Kim Yes . . .

Graham At a university?

Kim No . . . at the firm.

Graham Ah . . .

   Beat.

Do you get out of Moscow much?

Kim Yes, we have a place in the country.

Graham . . . That's nice.

Kim Yes, well, you have to really. The summers get terribly hot here. So ever since I found Rufa sitting in a bath of cold water to keep cool as she peeled potatoes, I've had a charming little dacha with all mod cons . . . Except hot water. But you don't really need that in the summer.

Graham . . . Where is it?

Kim Oh, only half an hour away . . . but the road stops at the edge of a forest, so we have no through traffic. Not even a serf on a tractor . . . In fact, the only real noise comes from our friendly woodpecker, which sounds off in five-second bursts exactly like a Bren gun . . .

He reflects.

Graham And do you ever go further afield?

Kim Yes. Within limits, of course. But we've been to Siberia – for our honeymoon – East Germany, Czechoslovakia, Bulgaria, and even Cuba once.

Graham (*interested*) Really?

Kim Yes, your old stomping ground. I was sorry I didn't meet Castro though . . . But I did see England on the way there.

Graham (*surprised*) What?

Kim Yes, the boat passed within sight of my old prep school at Eastbourne, though it was too foggy to get a really clear view.

Graham But how extraordinary. I dreamt you came to see me once. Perhaps it was on the same occasion?

Kim Perhaps.

Kim gets another drink.

By the way, I've been corresponding with that biographer of yours, Norman Sherry.

Graham Yes, so I understand . . . Thank you.

Kim Well, I've dredged up all I can remember of our time in MI6 together . . . But I haven't seen any of it in print yet, though I gather he's planning three volumes.

Graham Yes. He's been working on it for ten years and hasn't produced one yet. Not that it bothers me. The less said the better as far as I'm concerned.

Kim Quite . . .

Graham Poor chap though. Every time he goes anywhere he seems to get the same disease I got there. In Mexico, dysentery. In Panama, gangrene. In Liberia, tropical diabetes . . . I can't help feeling responsible . . .

Kim smiles.

Kim I have a Sherry too, actually. That chap Knightley, who spilt the beans, as you put it, about our letters . . .

Graham Oh yes . . .

Kim He wants to write another book about me, and to come and see me first.

Graham And will you let him?

Kim Probably. The secrecy doesn't seem to matter so much any more. And I can always dissimulate if necessary.

Graham Yes, you're good at that, aren't you?

He smiles.
  Then drinks.
  Kim looks at him.

Kim Tell me, Graham, why did you really come here?

Graham hesitates.

Graham How do you mean?

Kim Just for old times' sake?

Graham No, not just. I wanted to see you again. And to talk to you. I haven't had a chance to since I discovered you had a secret life . . . I want to try and understand you.

Kim Understand me?

Graham Yes.

Kim Why?

Graham . . . I'm curious. I am a writer, after all.

Kim thinks.

Kim You're not planning to write another novel about me, are you?

Graham No. I'm through with spy novels.

Kim Or an article? That might be worse.

Graham No . . . I promise.

Kim looks at him.

I just wanted to see you again.

Beat.

And you needn't worry about what you tell me as I'm bound to forget it in any case. I forget everything these days . . .

Kim smiles.

Kim Very well. Ask me what you like then.

Graham . . . Thank you.

Kim I can always refuse to answer.

Graham Yes . . .

Kim And what harm could there be at our age anyway?

Graham Exactly.

Kim raises his glass.

Kim In vodka veritas.

They smile and drink.
Graham thinks.

Graham All right . . . Why did you become a Communist?

Kim God, you sound just like Knightley.

Graham Sorry. It's the journalist in me.

Kim Yes . . . But in any case, I never know how to answer that question.

Graham You don't think it had anything to with your father then?

Kim You mean he turned against the British and became a Muslim spy for Ibn Saud, so I turned against them and became a Communist spy for Stalin?

Graham Yes . . .

Kim No, I don't. My conversion came at Cambridge.

Graham Through that Marxist don, you mean?

Kim Partly. But it was more just the whole atmosphere of the place. It was the time of the hunger marches to London, and the rise of the Nazis after all, though I'm ashamed to say I actually canvassed for the Labour Party once . . . So there was no epiphany. I just gradually became convinced that Communism was the only answer, and straight after my finals I went to Vienna to fight against the fascist regime of Dollfuss. And there met Litzi, who became my first wife.

Graham Litzi?

Kim Yes.

Graham I always thought Aileen was your first wife.

Kim Well, she wasn't. She was my second wife.

Graham So who was Litzi?

Kim Litzi was an Austrian Jewish Communist, and the divorced daughter of the family I lodged with in Vienna . . . At our first meeting she asked me how much money I had, and I said a hundred pounds, which I hoped would last me about a year. But she made some calculations and announced, 'That will leave you an excess of twenty-five pounds. You can give that to the International Organisation for Aid for Revolutionaries. We need it desperately.'

Graham smiles.

Well, I fell in love with her there and then. And began to work with her. Begging people for money, acting as a courier for underground organisations, helping hunted militants to get out of Vienna . . .

He reflects.

We first made love on a side street in the snow . . . Hard to believe it now, but it was actually quite warm once you got used to it . . . Anyway, it was a memorable way to lose your virginity.

He smiles.

Then when the fascist crackdown on revolutionaries got too intense, I felt I had to get her out of the country. So I married her and took her back to London with me . . . And it was shortly after my return that I was approached.

Beat.

Graham How?

Kim Litzi came home one evening and told me that she had arranged for me to meet a man of 'decisive importance'. I remember her words exactly. Of course I questioned her about it but she refused to give me any details, other than that I was to meet him at a particular time at a bench in Regent's Park . . . So I turned up and met a small, stout man with curly hair, who said his name was Otto, though I later discovered it was –

He checks himself.

Actually, I'd better not say.

Graham smiles.

Graham Very well. Tell me about 'Otto'.

Kim thinks back.

Kim Well, the first thing you noticed about him were his eyes. He looked at you as if nothing more important in life than you – and talking to you – existed at that moment . . . And he spoke at great length, arguing that a person with my background could do far more for Communism than the run-of-the-mill Party member . . . Then he asked me if I'd like to join the Russian intelligence service, and I accepted, without hesitation. One does not look twice at an offer of enrolment in an elite force.

He looks at Graham.

Graham Go on.

Kim Well, his first instructions were that I should immediately break off all contact with my Communist friends, and that I should become, to all outward appearances, a conventional member of the class I was committed to opposing . . . Then he gave me a Minox subminiature camera and a codename, and began to instruct me in the rudiments of tradecraft. How to arrange a meeting, where to leave messages, how to detect if my telephone was bugged, how to spot a tail, how to lose one, and so forth . . . My first task was to spy on my father, as it was believed he had important secret documents in his office. So I photographed them with my camera and gave the film to Otto.

Graham You spied on your father?

Kim Yes. But I don't believe there was anything in them, as no one in Britain would have trusted my father by then in any case. They were just testing my commitment . . . For the next two years I was then given virtually nothing to do. But in the long term I was given the job of penetrating British intelligence and told it did not matter how long it took me to do it.

Beat.

Graham What about Litzi?

Kim Well . . . of course, once I'd been recruited, Litzi and I had to split up, for the good of our work, so as not to endanger each other.

He reflects sadly.

Graham Tough . . .

Kim Yes . . . The last time I saw her was in Vienna just after the war – just before you filmed *The Third Man* there – when I had to go and see her to get a divorce.

Graham That was pretty risky, wasn't it?

Kim That's what I thought. So I told MI6 first, and fortunately they believed that my marriage to a Communist was just a youthful aberration.

He smiles.

She lives in East Berlin now and is happily married to another Communist. At least I assume she's happy. She has a daughter anyway.

Graham thinks.

Graham I can understand why you agreed to work for the Russians in the early thirties, but why did you carry on after Stalin's Pact with Hitler? Surely you saw that as a betrayal?

Kim Well, it was certainly a surprise. But I still had faith that Uncle Joe was playing the long game and was just neutralising Hitler in the short term to win time.

Graham And divide up Poland . . .

Kim He needed a buffer . . . But as it happens, I did stop for a while, as I was worried that secrets I'd been providing about the British and French armies might be passed on to the Germans – that was when I was working as a foreign correspondent for *The Times*. But then, just before the Germans turned on Russia, I finally managed to get into MI6. At which point of course the KGB got in touch with me again.

Graham And MI6 never knew about your Communist past?

Kim Actually, they did. As part of the vetting process, the Vice Chief asked my father and me to lunch at his club. And when I was in the loo, he asked about the rumours that I had been a Communist at Cambridge. To which my father replied, 'Oh, that was all schoolboy nonsense. He's a reformed character now.'

He smiles.

And apparently the Vice told the Chief, 'Philby's clean. I know his people' . . . So I was in. On the word of my father. But then you were a Party member once, weren't you – which I never was – and you got in?

Graham That was different. I was a member for *four weeks* at Oxford when I was nineteen. It was just a joke. A prank with a friend to try to get ourselves a free trip to Moscow, which has caused me great problems with the Americans ever since . . . And it's taken me till now to finally get that trip, though as a writer rather than a Communist, of course.

Beat.

I suppose you got a free trip too.

Kim Well, I wouldn't describe it as free . . . and, of course, mine wasn't a return.

Graham No . . .

Beat.

Anyway, do go on.

Kim Well, you know the next bit, as that's when I met you, at your MI6 training. (*A thought strikes him.*) How *did* you get in?

Graham My sister, Elizabeth, recommended me. She'd already joined. And I've always had a taste for adventure. Not that I found much. Unlike you.

Kim Well, we did send you to Sierra Leone.

Graham Yes, and damn dull it was too.

Kim Really? I remember you setting up a roving brothel to catch the Vichy French and Germans spying on British shipping.

Graham Well, I had to do something to liven things up a bit . . . though it turned out the brothel market was already controlled by the French.

Kim So you came back to St Albans to work under me.

Graham Yes . . .

They think back.

Kim Remember those long boozy lunches we used to have?

Graham Of course . . . Halcyon days.

Kim Mm . . .

They remember fondly for a moment.

(*Pointedly.*) But when I became head of Russian counter-intelligence, you resigned, so I didn't see so much of you . . .

Graham No . . .

Kim waits for him to say more but he doesn't.

But that was quite a coup for you, wasn't it? Being given responsibility for catching yourself.

Kim Yes, I suppose it was. But it was a ridiculous situation. If all my operations had failed, I'd have lost my job. But obviously I couldn't let them all succeed either, as that would have harmed the Soviets.

Graham And catching Donald Maclean was one that had to fail?

Kim Of course. But that came later. After I was sent to Washington . . . Maclean had been there during the war, but it was only later that he was identified as the mole who had leaked the conversations between Churchill and Truman to Stalin.

Graham Right . . . So you warned him?

Kim No, actually. Guy Burgess did . . .

Graham is puzzled.

You see, Maclean was now in London. But Burgess was in Washington with me. Indeed, he was staying in my house. So Guy and I agreed that he would sail from New York the next morning to warn Maclean . . . Crucially though, Guy promised that he wouldn't go with Maclean to Moscow as that would compromise me.

Graham Of course.

Kim Well, about five days later, during a briefing, I learned that he had broken his promise, and as you can imagine, my consternation was no pretence . . . For the second time in my life, a Soviet shell had blown up right next to me.

Graham . . . How do you mean?

Kim When I was in Spain, a Republican shell landed next to a car I was in, and the other three journalists in it were all killed.

Graham Oh yes, I remember.

Kim Franco gave me a medal. And that's when I became known as 'Lucky Kim'. But this time, I wasn't quite so lucky . . .

He reflects.

Graham Why do you think Burgess went?

Kim I don't know. Perhaps he was ordered to . . . But I think he probably just got cold feet . . . Either way, the whole thing was a mess, an intelligence nightmare, and it was all due to him. He was the unpredictable factor. 'The human factor', as you would say . . .

He looks at him.

Why *did* you leave MI6, just when I offered you a promotion?

Graham hesitates.

Graham Because I thought at the time you'd ousted Cowgill for entirely selfish, career motives, and I didn't want any part of it . . . I didn't know you'd been ordered to supplant him.

Kim You hadn't realised I was working for the Russians then?

Graham No . . . of course not.

Kim looks sceptical.

Kim What would you have done if you had known?

Graham thinks.

Graham As a friend, I'd have given you twenty-four hours to get away and then reported you.

Kim Betrayed me?

Graham Of course. It would have been my duty.

Kim But I thought you took E. M. Forster's line that you'd rather betray your country than your friend?

Graham Yes, but there are limits.

Kim smiles briefly.

Kim Only twenty-four hours, eh? . . . So *The Third Man* wasn't my warning?

Graham . . . *The Third Man*?

Kim Yes. Orson Welles's character, Harry Lime . . . I took him to be me.

Graham Really . . . Why?

Kim Well . . . just think of the story for a moment . . . The villain is the hero's old friend, only he is not who he seems, but is really operating on the wrong side of the law . . . And he's called Harry.

Graham So?

Kim My first name is Harold. H. A. R. Philby, remember? Harold Adrian Russell.

Graham So it is . . .

Kim Kim was just my father's nickname for me.

Graham After Kipling's spy novel?

Kim Yes . . .

Graham And you think your father had no influence on you?

Kim I didn't say that.

Beat.

And then the climax, Harry trying to escape through the sewers of Vienna . . .

Graham Yes?

Kim It was me who told you about those sewers, since that's how we used to get people out when I was fighting the fascists there in '33.

Graham You told me that?

Kim Yes, in the King *Harry* pub in St Albans, which we used to go to when we worked in that house in King *Harry* Lane during the war . . .

Graham But why would you have told me that if you were trying to keep your Communist past a secret?

Kim I thought I could trust you. And it was my Communist present that was the real secret.

Graham thinks.

Graham Well, certainly, the hero, Holly Martins, is a thriller writer like I am . . .

Kim He writes Westerns, actually.

Graham rethinks.

Graham Oh yes, so he does.

Kim But the point holds. You were Holly Martins, the writer hero, and I was Harry Lime, the bad guy, Harry being my first name.

Graham Mm . . .

Graham considers this.

But then Harry's slang for Henry too, isn't it? Which is my first name.

Kim . . . Is it?

Graham Yes. Henry Graham Greene . . . And, of course, 'lime' is a kind of green. So you could say Harry Lime is me, Henry Greene.

Kim looks troubled.

27

Graham But did I ever tell you what David Selznick said about Harry and Holly?

Kim No, I don't believe you did.

Graham Oh. Well, Carol Reed and I went to Hollywood to discuss the script, and Selznick says (*Hollywood mogul accent.*) 'What's all this buggery?' (*Normal voice.*) 'Buggery?' I said. 'Yes', he said. 'Chap goes out to find his friend. Doesn't find him. He's apparently dead. Why doesn't he go home?' . . . I said, 'Well, look . . . he's got a motive of revenge. He's been assaulted by the British military police. He's fallen in love with a girl.' 'Yes, but that's after twenty-four hours. Why didn't he go home before that? . . . It's buggery, boys. Sheer buggery. It's what you learn at those English public schools of yours.'

He smiles.

He had a point, I suppose. Holly does love Harry in a way . . .

Kim Yes . . . But then at the end, when he discovers Harry's betrayal, he helps the police catch him . . .

Graham True . . .

Beat.

Is that why you dropped me after Burgess and Maclean went? Because you thought I suspected you?

Kim Yes. They *were* looking for 'The Third Man', after all, as the press never stopped telling us.

Graham But I couldn't have known you'd become the *Third* Man when I wrote it, three years before Burgess and Maclean disappeared.

Kim No . . . that was uncanny . . . almost as if you'd had a premonition . . .

He reflects.

But I also didn't want to cause you any trouble.

Graham Why would you have caused me trouble?

Kim Because you were famous by then. You'd written *The Third Man*. And *The Heart of the Matter*. And *The End of the Affair*. And I was under suspicion. Being interrogated indeed. So you had a lot to lose. And I didn't want you to lose it by association with me.

Graham But I'd left MI6 years ago. And in any case, I didn't know you were . . . well, guilty.

Kim Didn't you? Even then?

Graham No. I was inclined to side with you. As all your friends were. Nick Elliot, Muggeridge, Trevor-Roper . . . We thought you were just paying the price for your loyalty to, and friendship with, Burgess. And we rather admired you for it.

Kim Well, I'm touched to hear it. But I understood differently. That you knew I was . . . guilty, as you put it.

Graham Why?

Kim Because of *The Third Man*. I distinctly remember the chill that went down my spine when I first saw it . . . And because you were smarter than everyone else. In terms of human psychology, I mean. You were a novelist after all. And our best, in my opinion.

Graham Thank you . . . And in my opinion, you were our best spy. Or rather, *their* best spy.

He smiles.

But I'm sorry my film caused you such discomfort. It wasn't intended, I assure you. Or at least, not consciously. I was just trying to write a good screenplay.

Beat.

Kim Yes, well, perhaps being the most wanted man in England made me a little paranoid.

Graham Yes . . . I suppose it might.

Pause.

But none of this explains why it says 'Martins' on your buzzer?

Kim is surprised.

I saw it when I came in.

Kim . . . How observant of you.

Beat.

Anyway, it's my name.

Graham Your name?

Kim Yes, my Russian name. Andrei Fedorovich Martins.

Graham It doesn't sound very Russian.

Kim No. Well, it wasn't my first choice . . . My first Soviet passport gave my name as Andrei Fedorovich Fyodorov, Fyodorov being a fairly common name here . . . But then one day I had toothache and went to the dentist, where the receptionist asked me my name. 'F-Fyodorov,' I stuttered with much effort, not helped by my toothache. The woman burst out laughing. (*Russian accent.*) 'Fyodorov?' she demanded. 'Just look at you. Who would take you for a Russian? Fyodorov indeed.' And she poked fun at me with her finger . . . After that I became Andrei Fyodorovich Martins and said I was a Latvian born in New York. But I never got used to it. Rufa would call out 'Andrei Fyodorovich!' in the street from time to time and I wouldn't even turn my head.

Graham But that still doesn't explain why you chose the name Martins, the hero in *The Third Man*? Was it a reference to your being 'The Third Man'?

Kim No. It was a reference to my being the hero, and as innocent and well-meaning as he is. Or at least, not as corrupt, amoral and self-serving as Harry Lime.

Graham . . . I see.

Beat.

Kim But of course, after Burgess and Maclean went, I had to leave MI6, even if most people did think I was innocent.

Graham nods.

Graham And you didn't confess . . . ?

Kim No, though I was put under a lot of pressure to . . . But a spy should never confess.

Graham takes this in.

Graham What did you do next?

Kim For the next few years, not a lot . . . But having failed to get back into journalism, everything changed when that Labour MP named me in the Commons and I was suddenly besieged by journalists.

He smiles.

I remember it was a busy time for them in my part of Sussex. Princess Margaret's romance with Group Captain Townsend was also in the news, so the reporters used to doorstep Margaret at Uckfield in the morning, Townsend down the road at Eridge in the afternoon, and if they had time, squeeze me in at Crowborough, midway between the two, around lunchtime.

Graham But then Macmillan cleared you?

Kim Yes. Well, he had to really, without a confession. And after that, the way was clear for me to get back into MI6, and I was sent to Beirut, working for the *Observer* and the *Economist* as cover.

Graham Where you met Eleanor?

Kim Yes . . .

Beat.

She was married to the *New York Times* correspondent, Sam Brewer, at the time. So I guess you could say I screwed America in more ways than one. Or perhaps we were just confirming the Special Relationship? . . . Anyway, when her divorce came through, I told Sam that I wanted him to be the first person to know I was going to marry his ex-wife. To which he replied – (*American accent.*) 'That sounds like the best solution. What do you make of the situation in Iraq?'

Graham smiles.

Graham That was decent of him.

Kim I thought so.

He reflects.

So everything was going swimmingly . . . until George Blake was lured back to England and given forty-two years, the longest term ever imposed under English law . . . Well, you can imagine the effect that had on me, knowing that I might be next . . .

Graham Yes . . .

Kim And then, of course, my old friend, Nick Elliott, came out to Beirut and confronted me with the new and conclusive evidence against me . . .

Graham . . . Which was?

Kim The testimony of a woman called Flora Solomon, who'd introduced me to Aileen when they worked together at Marks and Spencer in the thirties, and whom I'd once unwisely tried to recruit.

Graham is puzzled.

Graham But why had she only come forward now?

Kim I believe she'd taken against my pro-Arab articles in the *Observer*. She was an ardent Zionist. And of course, she already blamed me for abandoning Aileen and the children.

Graham And they confronted you out there for fear that if they tried to lure you back to England, you'd abscond before they could get a confession?

Kim Presumably. Unless, of course, they *wanted* me to go to Russia to avoid the scandal of another court case . . . But I'll probably never know the answer to that.

Graham thinks.

Graham How did you escape?

Kim My contact got me on a Russian cargo ship. But it was a close-run thing. And if the chap they'd sent out to interrogate me further hadn't stopped off on his way for a four-day skiing holiday, I might never have made it. He'd been an Olympic skier, you see, and apparently the conditions in Lebanon were particularly good that year.

Graham Lucky Kim . . .

Kim Yes . . . You know I even thought of calling my book that. But we decided it wasn't serious enough.

Graham Yes, well, *My Silent War* certainly has more gravitas . . . But what happened when you arrived in Russia?

Kim smiles at the memory.

Kim Let me set the scene for you . . .

He thinks back.

It's five o'clock in the morning at a small port on the Black Sea in mid-winter. There's a table and a few chairs. A charcoal stove. Tea is brewing on the stove and the air is thick with cigarette smoke . . . Awaiting me are three or four militia men and a man from the service who speaks English, sent specially down from Moscow to meet me . . . After the formalities are over, I apologise for coming, and say I had wanted to stay on in the West and continue to serve but the pressure had become too much for me.

He pauses.

Well, my colleague from Moscow must have seen that I was a bit emotional about it all, as he put his hand on my arm and spoke to me. And I remember his exact words . . . He said, 'Kim, your mission has been concluded. We have a saying in our service that once counter-espionage becomes interested in you, it's the beginning of the end. We know that British counter-espionage became interested in you in 1951. It's now 1963 – twelve years. My dear Kim, what on earth are you apologising about?' . . . Those words of kindness, when I was at my most vulnerable, meant a lot to me . . .

Pause.

Graham And when you got to Moscow, did you see Burgess?

Kim No. He died just after I got here . . . I later found out he'd heard I was in Russia and asked to see me, but they told him I wasn't in Moscow . . . And I didn't know he was in hospital until it was too late . . .

Graham That seems cruel.

Kim I know . . . but I think they wanted to keep us apart to avoid recriminations over his part in my exposure.

Graham Or because they didn't want him to tell you how much he hated living here when you'd only just arrived?

Kim Perhaps . . . Anyway, I didn't get to see him before he died. Which I'm sorry about. I would like to have seen him one last time. He'd been a good friend . . .

He reflects.

Graham But you saw Maclean?

Kim Yes. With Guy gone, I was rather thrown together with Donald . . . And Melinda, of course . . .

They exchange a knowing glance.

Eleanor hadn't joined me yet . . .

Graham No . . . And when she did?

Kim Well, it quickly became apparent she wasn't really suited to life in Moscow. She asked me what was more important to me, her or the Communist Party? So I said, 'The Party, of course.' And that was the end really . . . She said I should only have married a dedicated Communist.

Graham And now you have . . .

Kim Yes, well, I'm not sure I'd describe Rufa as dedicated . . . Not like Litzi . . . In any case, Eleanor left shortly after. But it was perfectly amicable. I gave her my old Westminster scarf as a memento. It was the most valuable possession I had. And she left a note saying she'd come back if I ever lived in a city without Melinda. But instead, Melinda moved in with me, and by the time she moved out, Eleanor was dead, from cancer.

Graham nods.

But it was rather touching what she wrote about me in her book, *The Spy I Loved* . . . She said I'd had the guts to stand by a decision I'd made thirty years ago . . . And then I published my book, to which you so kindly agreed to write the foreword . . . And finally, of course, I met Rufa . . .

Graham So you've now had four wives of four different nationalities. Austrian, English, American and now Russian . . .

Kim Yes. But always with a higher loyalty.

Beat.

So there you have it. My entire life story . . .

He reaches for his glass and drinks.

Graham And you're happy here?

Kim Yes . . .

Beat.

Why wouldn't I be? . . . I'm honoured and respected, with numerous state decorations . . . The Order of Lenin, The Order of the Military Red Star, The Order of the Friendship of the Peoples, The Order of the Patriotic War First Class . . . My work, such as it is these days, proceeds reasonably satisfactorily within the restraints imposed by my chosen profession – not that I chose it myself, but I cannot think that those who chose it for me did wrong . . . And my private life is as rich a mixture as I can take. No tedious social obligations, and enough travel to make me appreciate the home comforts that await my return . . . My former pupils come to see me sometimes . . . and now I have even realised my old wish to have Graham Greene sitting across a table from me with a bottle of wine between us.

He smiles.

Or rather, vodka.

He drinks.

Graham And you've always been happy here?

Kim Yes . . . Indeed, I would say my time in Russia has been the happiest of my life.

He reflects.

And do you know what the most remarkable thing is? The stammer that had tortured me since I was a child – do you remember it?

Graham Of course.

Kim Well, the moment I got here, it disappeared. It was as if a huge weight had been lifted from my shoulders. As if all the stress and strain I'd been under for all those years, even before I was recruited, had somehow been released and I was free and home at last.

Beat.

Graham Then why did you try to kill yourself?

Kim is taken aback.

The scar on your wrist . . .

Kim looks at it.

I couldn't help noticing it as you reached for your glass.

Beat.
    Then Rufa enters.

Rufa Right . . .

She takes in the scene.

Dinner is ready.

Graham Ah . . . good.

They leave the room, Rufa first, followed by Graham and finally Kim.
    The lights fade as the 'Second Theme' from The Third Man *plays.*

Act Two

The same, later in the evening.
The 'Café Mozart Waltz' from The Third Man *plays as the lights come up on Graham and Rufa sitting down with glasses of red wine.*
The music fades.

Graham Does he always do the washing-up?

Rufa No. I do it usually. But then he usually cooks.

Graham Ah.

He smiles and sips his wine.

Rufa And it's very unusual for him to let me cook for anyone else. But he was so keen to have a proper talk with you.

Graham Yes, well . . . we had a lot to catch up on . . .

He reflects.

Rufa Yes . . .

Pause.

Of course, he prepared everything in advance.

Graham is perplexed.
Rufa sees this.

For the dinner.

Graham Oh yes . . . of course.

He smiles.

The perfect husband . . .

She considers this.

Rufa I wouldn't go that far.

He smiles again.
Then sips his wine.

Graham How did you two get together? If you don't mind my asking.

Rufa Why should I mind?

Graham is stumped.

I was working as an editor at the Central Economic-Mathematical Institute in Moscow when my friend there, Ida, invited me to an American Ice Show . . . Her husband, George, turned out to be an Englishman and he invited Kim, though Kim didn't manage to get a ticket in the end . . .

Beat.

Kim made no particular impression on me and I had no idea then that he and George were both involved with the KGB. I just saw an old man with a kind but rather flabby face . . . But he later told me that he knew from that moment, as he and George walked behind me and Ida to the stadium, that he was going to marry me. 'How did you know?' I asked. And he said, 'If you could only see the way you walked.'

Graham smiles.

Graham And this was when?

Rufa In the summer of 1970 . . . Then I met him properly at the Blakes' dacha in Tomilino . . .

She thinks back.

Ida had told me that he was an attractive man but with a weakness – a fondness for the bottle . . . And she also said he'd had an affair with Melinda Maclean but she thought that was over now . . .

Beat.

Anyway, of course, Kim brought all the ingredients for the meal himself and insisted on preparing it all himself too, and it was a great success. So I think it was his coq au vin that did it.

She smiles.

Graham That's what attracted you to him?

Rufa Yes. And his nice English manners. Not like Russian men . . . And his sense of humour, of course.

Graham Yes . . . that's what drew me to him too. The legendary charm . . .

He reflects.
Rufa misunderstands.

Rufa You were lovers?

Graham smiles.

Graham No. That wasn't our style. Unlike so many we knew . . . Though I suppose I did love him in a way . . .

Beat.

And of course I looked up to him enormously. Everyone did. He would have been C, you know, had things turned out differently.

Rufa C?

Graham Head of MI6.

Rufa Oh.

Beat.

Graham But what happened after the coq au vin?

Rufa Well, he then invited me with the Blakes to supper with his case officer at the time, Stanislav, and sat me at the head of the table as 'mistress of the house', though of course he had done all the cooking. And shortly after, I moved in as part of the family.

Graham The family?

Rufa Yes. The KGB family . . . And a few days later Kim phoned Stanislav and said he intended to marry me, so it was a *fait accompli* . . . Stanislav and Kim's other case officer were the witnesses at our wedding.

Graham takes this in.

The hard part though was saying goodbye to all but a couple of my friends . . . You see, when I married Kim, I had to cut myself off from them because I was not allowed to tell them my husband's name, nor give them our address. And I couldn't explain why either, so naturally some of them were hurt . . . But of course Kim had to do this when he joined the family, and again when he defected. And I can tell you that he took it hard too. Because, whatever people may say, he values friendship very much . . . Not to mention the marriages it cost him . . .

Graham Yes . . .

A thought strikes her.

Rufa I suppose you must have known his second wife, Aileen?

Graham Yes . . . a little.

Rufa . . . What was she like?

Graham Well, I only met her a few times and there always seemed to be young children about, but she seemed nice enough.

Rufa She used to hurt herself with scissors and things, no?

Graham So I gather . . . but she must have been under a great deal of strain . . .

Rufa Because of Kim's work, you mean.

Graham Yes.

Rufa Mm . . .

Beat.

Kim doesn't like to talk about his life before he came here, his personal life I mean . . . Once I saw Eleanor's book in his study and said I'd like to read it, but he snatched it out of my hands, and after that I never saw it again . . .

Graham Well . . . I guess he likes to keep things separate . . . Like Kipling's 'Two-Sided Man' . . .

Rufa Kipling . . .? He wrote that book Kim got his name from, didn't he?

Graham Yes. And in it there's a poem which fits our Kim too, I think . . . who also spent his first years in India, of course . . .

Rufa Go on . . .

Graham Well, I only remember the first verse.

He pauses.

'Something I owe to the soil that grew –
More to the life that fed –
But most to Allah Who gave me two
Separate sides to my head.'

Rufa considers this.

Rufa Only two?

He smiles.

Graham And, of course, Kim never became a Muslim, unlike his father.

Rufa No . . . Kim does not believe in any kind of God . . .

Graham reflects.

Graham No . . .

He sips his red wine.
  She hesitates.
  Then makes a decision.

Rufa Graham, as you are one of Kim's oldest friends, and the only one who has come to see him here in Russia, there is something I want to tell you. But you must promise not to tell anyone else.

Graham thinks.

Graham Very well.

Beat.

Rufa Kim is dying.

Pause.

No one else knows. Apart from the doctors, of course. Kim doesn't even know.

Graham takes this in.

But I've been wanting to tell someone for months and it seems right that it should be you.

Beat.

Graham What's wrong with him?

Rufa His heart is very weak and the doctor says he cannot last more than another year at most. He's already lived longer than they expected . . . So thank you for coming to see him. It is just in time.

Graham . . . I will come again soon. If possible.

Rufa smiles.

Rufa Thank you. I know seeing you has given him great joy.

Pause.
  Then Kim enters holding a bottle of wine.

43

Kim Now, time for another bottle of our best Georgian, don't you think?

Graham Yes . . .

Rufa You have already had a lot. But perhaps it doesn't matter. With Graham being here, I mean.

Kim Exactly. It's a special occasion.

He uncorks the wine before refilling their glasses.

So, what have you been talking about while I've been washing up?

Rufa and Graham exchange glances.

Rufa I told Graham how we met.

Kim Ah . . . yes. Through the Blakes.

Graham Yes. Do you still see them?

Kim Sadly not. We fell out.

Graham Oh.

Rufa Yes, it is a great pity. They were our best friends. And it was all over a photograph.

Graham A photograph?

Kim Yes.

Beat.

You see, we used to spend a lot of time together – went on holiday and all that, you know – when one day George and Ida invited us over to their dacha for lunch. This would have been in the mid-seventies. Not all that long after Rufa and I married. But the thing was, my son, John, happened to be over from England and he was trying to make his way as a photographer. So when we were sitting outside round the table at lunch, he asked if he could take a picture of us all. And, anxious to help him in his career, I said yes. And much to my surprise, so did George. So John took these photographs of us . . . Then, of course, he went back to London and shortly afterwards these pictures were published all round the world. Or the Western world anyway. And George was furious. It seems he thought he'd only given his consent to the pictures being taken for private use. And he didn't like my son making money out of him. But he knew he was a photographer . . . Anyway, whatever the rights and wrongs of it, we haven't seen each other since.

Rufa Well, I still see Ida sometimes. But it is not the same.

Kim No . . .

Rufa So it is a great shame. And all over a silly photograph.

Pause.

Anyway, I'm going to leave you boys to chat while I go and watch the news. Perhaps you'll be on it, Graham?

Graham I doubt it. I think they were more interested in the film stars.

She smiles.

Rufa What time is your car coming?

Graham Eleven o'clock.

Rufa So I will come and take you back down then.

Graham Thank you.

She goes.
  Beat.

You have a charming wife.

Kim I know.

Kim refills Graham's glass before refilling his own.

Listen, about what you said before supper . . . I won't try and deny it. But I want you to know, that happened before I met Rufa.

Graham takes this in.

Graham Right . . .

Pause.

Well, it's really none of my business anyway . . . It's just that you said you were so happy here.

Kim Yes, well, I have been since I met her.

Beat.

But I admit that before that, in the late sixties, there was a difficult moment.

Pause.

It was after Melinda went back to Donald . . . and I was left on my own. Without anyone really. And nothing to do . . . For some reason, the firm wouldn't let me do any work for them at that point. And they wouldn't let me publish my book either . . . And then that *Sunday Times* book came out, *The Spy Who Betrayed a Generation* . . . and le Carré wrote that introduction. Do you remember?

Graham Yes . . .

Kim He said I had 'no home, no woman, no faith' . . . and that I was 'spiteful, vain and murderous'.

Graham Yes, he really doesn't like you, does he?

Kim No. He said they should have 'liquidated' me in Beirut.

Graham So I recall . . .

Beat.

Kim But it was personal, you see.

Graham How do you mean? Do you know him?

Kim No. But after I left, he had to leave the service and become a full-time writer.

Graham Well, that is a terrible fate, that's for sure . . .

Kim Yes, but unlike you, it wasn't voluntary.

Graham is puzzled.

Graham But I always thought he left after the success of *The Spy Who Came in from the Cold*?

Kim He did, but not *because* of it . . .

Graham doesn't understand.

He was based in Bonn, you see . . . Working for the firm.

Graham (*getting it*) And you gave his name to the Russians . . .

Kim . . . I've told you, I can't comment on operational matters. Though I hardly think it matters now.

Beat.

Anyway, despite all that, I admit that 'no home, no woman, no faith' line did sting a bit. Because there was an element of truth in it. Or that's how I felt at the time. And I wondered whether it had all been worth it. All the sacrifices I had made. All the deaths . . . Which is when the doubts set in . . . And I didn't have enough to do . . . so I turned in on myself . . .

Beat.

Stupid really, looking back on it.

Graham Well, I'm hardly one to criticise. I used to play Russian roulette.

Kim Yes, but at least you had the excuse of youth.

Graham hesitates.

Graham Not always, actually . . .

Kim is surprised.

In my late forties . . . after my marriage . . . and other failed relationships . . . I once swallowed three-quarters of a bottle of whisky, mixed with a quarter of a bottle of gin, and ten aspirins.

Kim takes this in.

I woke up fine, surprisingly . . .

He reflects.

But I sometimes think my whole life has been a game of Russian roulette . . . Throwing myself into war zones and other dangerous places all the time . . .

Kim Yes, well, neither of us made life easy for ourselves, did we?

Graham No . . .

Beat.

What went wrong in your relationship with the KGB?

Kim I'm not sure. My pay still arrived regularly . . . they just didn't give me anything to do.

Graham Did you complain?

Kim No . . . I just got very bored . . . and depressed . . . and drank a lot . . . you know . . .

Graham nods.

But things got better when they finally let me publish my book in the West, as a kind of reply to the *Sunday Times* book and le Carré . . . And then, of course, you agreed to write the foreword, when there was no one else in England to defend me. No one else on my side. And when I read it, I felt like I'd been understood at last.

Beat.

Why did you defend me and stick by me when no one else would? Despite the risk to your reputation.

Graham Because I realised that you'd been fighting for a cause you believed in, rather than just your own self-interest, so my old liking for you came back.

Kim Yes, but with all that it cost you. The Nobel Prize perhaps? A knighthood?

Graham I wouldn't accept a knighthood anyway. And as for the Nobel Prize, apparently there's a member of the committee who didn't approve of *The Power and the Glory* and has been blackballing me ever since. As a Catholic he didn't like the idea of the priest fathering a child.

Kim But you're a Catholic?

Graham Yes. But not a very good one. My faith isn't as strong as yours . . . In fact, you could say I'm a Catholic agnostic. But I keep a foot in the door.

Kim smiles.

Then there's my childhood of course . . .

Kim How do you mean?

Graham Put it this way, when your father is also your headmaster, you learn from a young age what it is to have divided loyalties . . .

Beat.

And besides, you weren't so hard to understand. To some degree, at least. After all, every novelist has something in common with a spy . . . He watches, he overhears, he seeks motives, analyses character . . . *invents* character, creates plots, pulls strings to manipulate events, tells elaborate lies which he calls stories, kills characters off . . . if necessary. All to serve his higher purpose, of course.

He smiles briefly.

He's unscrupulous. If he's any good.

Kim Or as you once said, there's a splinter of ice in the heart of a writer?

Graham Exactly.

Kim But a whole icicle in the heart of a spy . . .

Graham is uncomfortable.

That's what you wrote in my book.

Graham . . . Was I wrong? My work is only fiction. But in yours real lives are at stake.

Beat.

Kim I did what had to be done . . .

Pause.

But you're wrong if you think I didn't feel badly about it sometimes. Just as every decent soldier feels badly about killing in war . . .

Graham considers this.

Graham You must have some regrets though?

Kim . . . What are you asking for, Graham? My confession.

Graham No . . . I'm not a priest. Just the truth.

Beat.

Kim All right . . .

He thinks.

Professionally, I certainly could have done better. I made mistakes and paid for them. Chief amongst them my friendship with Guy . . . not to mention Flora Solomon . . .

Graham And morally?

Kim How do you mean?

Graham All those agents killed in operations because you tipped off the Russians. In Albania, Bulgaria, the Ukraine . . .

Kim looks at him.

Kim The agents we sent on all those operations were quite as ready as I was to contemplate bloodshed in the service of a political ideal. They were armed men intent on sabotage and murder. They knew the risks they were running . . . I, on the other hand, was serving the interests of the Soviet Union and those interests required that these men were defeated. To the extent that I helped defeat them, even if it caused their deaths, I have no regrets.

Beat.

Graham But you trained these men – who trusted you, saw you as a friend even – before you sent them to their deaths.

Kim War is a nasty business. And deception is part of it. That's what all this spying and intelligence business is all about . . . And besides, many of them were actually former Nazi collaborators, who'd been smuggled into the US after the war.

Graham Not the two young Georgians . . .

Kim hesitates.

Kim No . . . I admit, not them . . .

He reflects as he sips his Georgian wine.

Graham You remember them then?

Kim Of course . . .

He thinks back.

They were energetic lads, who'd just turned twenty . . . Their parents had left Georgia after the Revolution and they'd both been born in Paris, so they knew of Georgia only by hearsay. But they spoke Georgian . . . From Paris they went to London for training in elementary diversionary techniques and six weeks later they were brought to me in Istanbul . . . I then accompanied them to Erzurum . . . There I gave them gold coins and provisions before handing them over to Turkish Intelligence, who took them to the Turko-Soviet border . . .

Beat.

Upon their return, the Turks said that soon after the young men had stepped onto Soviet territory, they heard shots . . . One of the young men fell. The other they saw running through the forest . . .

Pause.

It was an unpleasant business . . . The boys weren't bad. Not at all. And I knew very well that they would be caught and that a tragic fate awaited them . . . But it was the only way of driving a stake through the plans for future operations. So I have no regrets.

Beat.

Graham You still have your chilling certainty?

Kim On those matters, yes.

Graham takes this in.

Graham I could never have been a double agent . . .

Kim (*sharply*) I was never a double agent. I was a straightforward penetration agent.

Graham Or a straightforward traitor?

Kim is surprised.

Kim You can't betray what you never belonged to . . . At the age of twenty-one I committed myself to Communism. I was then given the task of getting into the security service. So it was up to them to know what I was doing.

He drinks.
  A tense pause.

At the end of *The Third Man*, Holly Martins kills his old friend Harry Lime, who he blames for the death of many innocent people . . .

Graham Yes . . .

Kim Well then. You haven't come to kill me, have you?

  Graham smiles.

Graham No.

Kim Good . . .

  Beat.

Then we're still friends?

Graham Of course.

  Kim smiles.

Kim I'm glad to hear it . . . Especially as you are, in fact, my only friend . . . Besides Rufa, of course . . .

  Graham considers this.

Graham Really?

Kim Yes. Think about it . . . Guy was my friend, but he died before I could see him. Though he did leave me all his books, and this chair, in his will . . . Then Donald and Melinda were my friends, but I rather messed that up, didn't I? . . . And George was a friend, until we fell out over that photograph . . . And all my other English friends have deserted me. Nicholas Elliott . . . well, hardly surprising I suppose after I left him high and dry in Beirut . . . I wrote and offered to meet him in Finland, you know, but he never responded . . . And there was my old school friend, Tim Milne, who also joined the firm . . . but, well, I did give his name to Elliott to try and put him off the scent of the real

53

people he was looking for, so it's not surprising I haven't heard from him since either . . . And then, of course, there was Hugh Trevor-Roper, who also never replied to my letter and wrote that nasty book about me . . .

Beat.

But I guess that's the price you pay if you deceive your friends, and believe me, it's a heavy one . . .

He pauses.

But I still think I was right to do it. Because to have refused to serve the cause I believed in to the best of my ability would have been to betray myself. And surely, that would have been the worst betrayal of all.

Pause.

So that just leaves you, Graham. Besides the journalists, and the minders, and the occasional ex-students who write to me from time to time . . . You are my last remaining friend . . . and I can't tell you how much it means to me to see you again after all these years.

Graham seems a little uneasy.

Graham Yes . . . well . . . me too.

Kim . . . It's good to know our friendship has survived all that has happened.

Graham Yes . . .

They drink.
Pause.

Of course, if you lived in England, we could see much more of each other . . .

Kim Yes . . . Or if you lived here . . .

He smiles.
Graham smiles back.
They finish their drinks.

54

Now, how about some whisky?

Graham hesitates.

Graham Why not?

Kim Good. I have some Scotch my son brought me.

He gets up and goes to the drinks cabinet.

Ah yes, here it is.

Kim pours out two glasses.
Beat.

Graham Do you ever miss it? England, I mean.

Kim thinks.

Kim Well, I miss seeing more of my children and grandchildren . . . And watching cricket at Lord's of course.

He takes the glasses back to the table and gives one to Graham.

I was quite a useful player at Westminster you know.

Graham Oh yes, what did you do? Bat or bowl?

Kim Bowl.

Graham And where did you field? Third man?

Kim smiles.

Kim No.

Beat.

Deep extra cover.

They laugh.
Then drink.

Graham (*appreciating the whisky*) Mm . . . But there must be other things you miss too?

Kim Not much . . . Coleman's mustard, Oxford coarse cut marmalade, Lea and Perrins Worcestershire sauce . . . Marmite, of course . . . but my family bring me those when they come and see me. You can bring me some next time you come too . . .

Graham smiles non-committally.

But although life here has its deprivations, it also has its advantages . . . I get great pleasure from the dramatic change in seasons . . . I even get pleasure from the search for scarce goods.

Graham But you're a privileged citizen. A general in the KGB.

Kim Strictly speaking, I have no military rank, but I do have the *privileges* of a general . . . The only one that really matters to me though is the first-class medical treatment I get, available quickly. Which, frankly, having been ill, I wouldn't want to be without.

Graham Sounds rather like Bupa . . .

Kim smiles uncomfortably.

So you've never thought of returning to England?

Kim No. I'm quite content here. Besides not wanting to be put in prison, of course.

Graham Yes. But what if you weren't put in prison . . .

Kim looks at him.
Beat.

Kim What do you mean?

Graham Well . . . if you were guaranteed immunity from prosecution?

They look at each other for a moment.
Then Kim smiles.

Kim And I thought you just wanted to see an old friend . . .

Graham I did . . . I just thought I'd better clear it with the firm first.

He smiles apologetically.

As I say, one never really leaves the firm entirely. Unless you defect to another one . . . Anyway, they asked me to give you their regards.

Kim Their regards?

Graham Yes. And an invitation. Now the Cold War seems to be thawing, they say they have no objection to your coming back. If you want to.

Kim That's what they said?

Graham Yes. Or words to that effect. The phrase 'water under the bridge' was used.

Beat.

Kim What about Rufa?

Graham Of course she would be welcome too.

Kim thinks.

Kim I see.

He smiles.

So it wasn't just curiosity, and friendship, and the Peace Conference that brought you here . . .

Graham Well, the Peace Conference brought me to Russia, and then when I mentioned it to the firm that I might go and see you, they asked me to test the water . . .

Kim To put out a feeler?

Graham Exactly.

Kim thinks it over.

Kim Yes, I can see it would be a bit of a coup for them, wouldn't it? And a slap in the chops for the Russians . . .

Graham can't deny it.
Pause.

What about the confession I made to Elliott in Beirut?

Graham . . . I thought a spy should never confess?

Kim He shouldn't. Unless it's necessary to allow time for an escape.

Graham Ah.

Kim And I confessed very little anyway. As I said, my activities ended with the beginning of the Cold War . . . Nevertheless, it could be used to prosecute me. As Blake's was. And unlike Blake, I'd be too old to escape.

Graham They don't have it.

Kim doesn't understand.

Kim But he taped it . . .

Graham Yes, but it's no good. The tape is inaudible. Too much noise from the traffic outside apparently . . . You see, he forgot to close the window.

Kim takes this in.
Then laughs.

Kim Poor Nick. No wonder he had to leave the service. And refused to meet me in Finland.

Graham Well, he was rather sore.

Kim . . . What's he doing now?

Graham Advising Margaret Thatcher on intelligence matters.

Kim smiles.

Actually, I'm not sure I should have told you that.

Kim Don't worry. It won't go any further.

Graham doesn't quite believe him.

Graham Anyway . . . the point is, you can come home if you want to.

Beat.

Kim Home . . .?

He considers this.

Thank you . . . but no. This is my home. And has been since I was twenty-two, when I threw in my lot with Otto . . . Even though I didn't get here till I was fifty . . .

He thinks back.

And it would be terribly ungrateful, don't you think?

Beat.

And might even make some people think I'd been working for the British all along . . . as a kind of triple agent . . . though in fact it would only make me a double, as I've explained . . .

Graham considers this possibility and is suddenly unsure.

Graham And you aren't?

They look at each other for a moment.

Kim No . . . of course not.

He smiles.

I'm not that tricky.

Graham smiles uncertainly.

Graham Well, that's a relief. As I'd feel rather a fool if you were, having gone into print defending you as a kind of latter-day Elizabethan martyr . . . Not to mention coming all this way to see you . . .

Kim I thought you said you'd come for the Peace Conference?

Graham Yes, well . . . I'm killing two birds with one stone really.

Kim Ah . . .

Pause.

In any case, it's too late.

He takes out a cigarette.

For me to move, I mean.

Beat.

Graham Why?

He lights his cigarette.

Kim Because I'm dying.

He smokes.

Graham Aren't we all at our age?

Kim smiles.

Kim Perhaps. But I've been given a deadline . . . as it were . . . of a year or so . . . Something to do with my heart.

Graham doesn't know what to say.

Graham I'm sorry.

Kim Thank you.

Beat.

But don't tell Rufa . . . She knows but thinks I don't.

He reflects.

It's easier that way.

Beat.

Graham And you don't want to die in England?

Kim No. That would be to deny my faith . . .

Graham takes this in.

Graham Very well. I'll pass that on.

Kim Thank you.

He puts the cigarette out.

It's funny. I am no longer a spy. Once your cover is blown, you are an ex-spy. 'A burnt-out case', as you would say . . . But you still have your cover as a novelist in place. So, between the two of us, it is you who is the spy now.

Graham can't deny it.

I thought it was odd your coming here after all these years . . . And so it is. After all, here you are, pretending to be just a writer at a conference when you're really on a secret mission to tempt me back to England.

Graham . . . I did just want to see you too.

Kim I dare say . . . but I wonder what the KGB would think . . .

Graham looks concerned.

Oh, you needn't worry. I shan't tell them. And I'm still glad you came.

Graham Good. So am I . . . I was just . . . passing on an invitation.

Kim . . . Quite.

Pause.

Graham Which reminds me of another, rather less important one . . .

Kim Oh yes?

Graham Yes . . . My sister and I want to start a club for old spies. There are so many of us in the South of France, we thought we should have a kind of Union. And I thought you might like to join?

Kim . . . Would I have to do anything?

Graham No. Just keep in touch occasionally . . . It's a shame Burgess and Maclean and Blunt are all dead. But we can ask Cairncross, who lives near me. And Blake, of course.

Kim Ah, yes, well, I'm not sure he'll be in. After the photograph incident.

Graham No . . .

Kim thinks.

Kim But I don't see why I shouldn't. So, yes, count me in.

Graham Excellent . . .

He smiles.

We can consider this the founding meeting.

Kim But I'm not sure we have a quorum, do we?

Graham Why not? Surely you only need two for a meeting of the Old Spies' Club?

Kim If you say so.

They smile.

I'll be secretary of the Moscow branch.

Graham Of course.

Kim Good. I'll ask Vladimir to join.

Graham Vladimir?

Kim My minder.

Graham Ah . . .

Graham thinks.

But if he's your minder, why isn't he here now?

Kim Oh . . . well . . . he is, actually.

Graham is surprised.

Next door in the study.

Graham takes this in.

Graham You mean he's been listening to everything we've been saying?

Kim No . . . I shouldn't think so. He's a great reader, is Vladimir.

Graham is still uneasy.

Graham Well, should I go and say hello to him?

Kim He'd rather you didn't. He doesn't like to intrude.

Beat.

And he keeps a low profile with Westerners especially.

Graham nods.

Graham Is he always here?

Kim Oh no. Just on special occasions.

Graham And this is a special occasion?

Kim Absolutely. You might have tried to kill me.

He smiles.

Or persuaded me to re-defect . . .

Graham looks uneasy.

Graham He won't mind about what I said, will he?

Kim You mean the invitation?

Graham Yes.

Kim No. I shouldn't think so. So long as I say no . . . It's all part of the game.

He smiles.
Graham is sufficiently reassured to take another sip of his whisky.
Then Rufa enters.

Rufa You were on the news, Graham.

Graham Really?

Rufa Yes. I caught a glimpse of you behind Gregory Peck.

Graham That's about right . . .

Rufa Oh yes, and Gorbachev said the Cold War is over. Apparently, we can no longer afford it.

They smile.
Pause.

Graham Anyway, I must be going. I'm giving a speech tomorrow.

Kim Oh yes. What on?

Graham Closer relations between Catholics and Communists.

Kim takes this in.

Kim Right . . .

Graham Not obvious bedfellows, I know . . . But both hate fascists, so that's one thing in common at least.

Kim Yes . . . good idea.

Rufa goes to the window and looks out behind the curtain.

Rufa I see your car is here.

Graham Oh good.

Rufa So I will come down with you.

Graham There's really no need.

Rufa It's not a problem. Now let's see if your shoes are dry.

She leads the way into the hall and takes the shoes from the radiator.

Ah yes. Perfectly.

Graham Thank you.

Rufa But you should wear boots next time.

Graham Yes . . .

Graham sits down and takes his slippers off.

Thank you for the slippers, Kim.

Kim Don't mention it.

Rufa helps him put his shoes on.
Kim passes the shoe horn.

The firm gave me that when I first arrived here. I'd never had a shoe horn before . . .

He reflects.

Rufa There we are.

Graham (*standing up*) I can see Kim is in good hands.

Rufa helps him on with his coat and smiles.

I mean you obviously look after him very well.

Rufa Yes. He is most fortunate.

Kim gives Graham his hat.
Meanwhile Rufa quickly slips on her boots and coat.
Kim and Graham look at each other for a moment.
Then embrace.

Kim Thank you for coming.

They separate.
Then look at each other.

Graham Say goodbye to Vladimir for me.

Kim nods.
Rufa looks at him, surprised.
Then Graham and Rufa turn to go.

Kim Oh, watch out for the ice. At night the path gets rather treacherous.

Graham smiles.

Graham I'll hold on to Rufa.

Kim Yes, that's what I do.

Kim looks at her fondly.
Then Graham and Rufa walk out of the flat as the lights cross-fade to them stepping into the lift.
Rufa pushes a button and they wait.

Rufa So, Kim has settled in well in Russia, no?

Graham Yes.

Rufa Though I do wish he had a friend like you here. But it's hard when his Russian is not good.

Graham Yes, I can imagine.

Rufa And it is sad when I come back from shopping or my mother's or a friend's, and see him at the window waiting for me.

She reflects.

You know once, after we'd had a row, I couldn't find one of my boots the next morning. And then he remembered he'd hidden it to stop me leaving.

She smiles sadly.

Did he tell you about his illness?

Graham . . . No.

Rufa Good. Then I think he doesn't know how serious it is . . . It is better like that.

Graham nods uncertainly.
Then they step out of the lift and she takes his hand as she leads him along the icy path.

Graham Did you know Vladimir was in the study?

Rufa Of course.

Graham And it doesn't bother you?

Rufa It used to. But you get used to it.

They stop at the roadside.

Well, goodbye, Graham.

She kisses him on both cheeks.

Come and see us again soon.

Graham nods non-committally.

Graham I'll try. And thank you for dinner. The coq au vin was delicious.

She smiles and walks back to the apartment block.
The lights change as Graham faces the audience.

Kim died the following year . . . of heart failure.

Beat.

Then they put him on a postage stamp . . . which would have pleased him, I think.

He reflects.

Within three years though, the Soviet Union – the country to which he had devoted his life and in which he never lost faith – ceased to exist . . . and perhaps he was fortunate not to witness that.

Beat.

'Lucky Kim' till the end . . .

Graham puts his hat on and walks off as The Third Man *returns and the lights cross-fade back to the living room.*
Kim sits in the green wingback chair with a glass of vodka.
He drinks deeply.
Then reflects.
The lights fade to black as the music finishes.
The End.